Class Teddy Bear

Belle Perez

My class has its own teddy bear.
His name is Ted.
We all take care of Ted.

We think Ted needs a hat.
The class likes this idea.

4

We make a paper hat for Ted.

We think Ted needs his arm fixed.
The class likes this idea.

6

We fix Ted's arm.

We think Ted needs a bed.
The class likes this idea.

8

We make a bed for Ted.

We think Ted needs a house.
The class likes this idea.

10

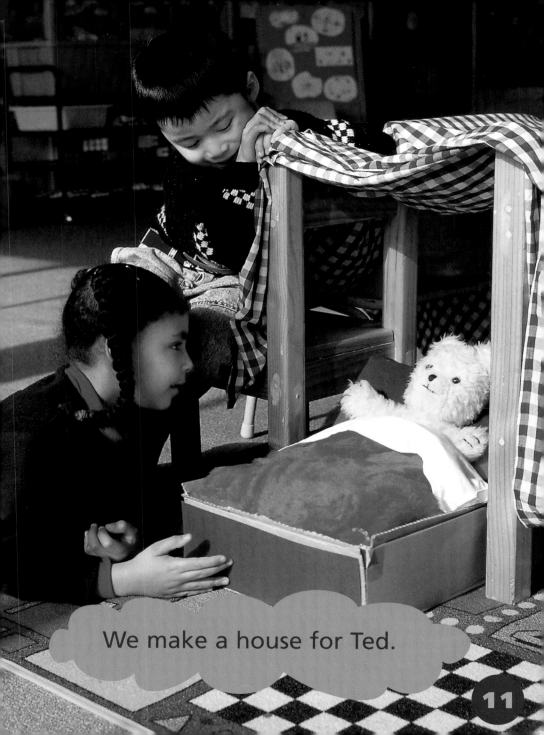

We make a house for Ted.

11